A Special Gift
for

_____

from

_____

_____

_____ *, 19* _____

Every effort has been made to contact the
various authors of writings in this book;
however, some could not be located and
are unknown to the writer and publisher.
Questions in this regard should be directed
to the publisher.

All writing in this book not otherwise
attributed is by the author.

Printed in the United States of America.

ISBN 0-915720-91-4

10 9 8 7 6 5 4 3 2 1

IT'S A One-derful LIFE

Written and Compiled by

MARY HOLLINGSWORTH

Foreword by LUCI SWINDOLL

Other Brownlow Gift Books

To Barbara, Charlotte, and Melva,
the Colorado Quartet and
Family Unit Five
with Love

It's a One-derful Life
is like a little treasure
you find in one of those old
bookstores out of the way and
around the corner. . .the kind of
book that surprises you with tidbits
of encouragement and hope.
The quotations alone make you
want to grab your friends,
sit them down and say,
"Listen to this, you're
gonna LOVE it."

Luci Swindoll

*O*PPORTUNITIES

Some opportunities come only when
you're alone, so being single can often
be a grand experience. When you're
single, you can curl up in front of a cozy
fire on a rainy day with a good book and
slip away into another world without
interruption. You can sing your favorite
song at the top of your voice in the shower,
and no one laughs. You can get down on
your knees in your room and tell God
what's on your heart in privacy and
openness with no eaves dropping.
You can stay up until the wee hours of
the morning watching Fred and Ginger
or Abbot and Costello with a dill pickle
and bowl of popcorn, and no one yells
at you to turn it down or turn off the light.
You can sit in a bubble bath until your skin
wrinkles up, and no one tells you to hurry.
Or you can write a book. You see, there
are some real advantages to being single.

Never look at
what you have lost.
Look at
what you have left.

—Robert Schuller

A NEW BEGINNING

I wish there were some wonderful place
  Called "The Land of Beginning Again,"
Where all our mistakes and our heartaches,
  And all of our poor selfish grief
Could be dropped like a shabby old coat
    at the door,
  And never be put on again.

—Louisa Fletcher

I am only one, but still I am one.
I cannot do everything, but still
I can do something; and because
I cannot do everything, I will not
refuse to do something that
I can do.

—Edward Everett Hale

*The greatest pleasure in life is
doing exactly what you thought
you couldn't do.*

—Unknown

INGLE

I know how it feels to be single, because I was single
all my life. I remember how lonely I was at times,
like the night in the garden. I really needed
someone to talk to, but my best friends just fell
asleep. Oh, they didn't mean to hurt me; they
were just so tired.

And I know what it's like to be tempted to do wrong
when you're alone. I was alone in the desert with
Temptation for forty days. I was weak and tired
and hungry, and Temptation knew just what to
do and say to make it easy for me to follow him.

I know how you feel when your friends turn their backs
on you in times of trouble. My friend Peter
turned his back on me when I was arrested and
wouldn't even admit that he knew me. It was as if
he was suddenly ashamed of me. I think he was
afraid of what would happen to him if he claimed
our friendship, considering the trouble I was in.
But, oh, how it hurt.

I understand your tears and feelings of despair when
you've lost someone you love, because my dear
friend Lazarus died. And I cried because it
broke my heart. He left such an empty place
in my life. Oh, yes, I know.

And I know the gripping fear of facing death alone,
because I faced a terrifying and painful death.
Even my own father turned his back on me and
left me there alone to die with two criminals.
I cried out, "Why, Father?" But he didn't even
answer. I died alone in the suffocating darkness.

But don't worry, my friend. I'll be there for you. I'll
listen when you need someone to talk to, and
I'll dry your tears and help you carry your
lonesome burdens. You can count on me.
I'll never leave you alone again, because
I know how it feels to be single.

*H*OPE

"*W*hen the hurts of today have drained
our endurance, and we are
crushed and broken by despair,
when we feel ourselves frozen in
an emotional paralysis that numbs
our senses so that nothing works,
our arms and legs hang limp and
even our eyes slump back into our
heads, we grope for the edge of
tomorrow. Its promise of a new
beginning is only a day away, and
its resource is hope. When we
think that we have nothing left,
we need to remember we still
have hope."

—Fay Angus
*Running Around
in Spiritual Circles*

Hope is the thing with feathers,
That perches in the soul,
And sings the tune without the words,
And never stops at all.

—Emily Dickinson

Opposites draw their meanings from
each other. Love is sweet because
of the bitterness of hate. Hope is
sunlight because of the darkness
of despair. You know joy's
exhilaration because you have felt
sorrow's depression.

Blessed are those whose dreams
are shaped by their hopes...
not by their hurts!

—Robert Schuller
The Be (Happy) Attitudes

PURPOSE

"Would you tell me, please,

which way I ought to go from here?"

said Alice to the Cat in *Alice in Wonderland.*

"That depends a good deal on where you

want to get to," said the Cat.

"I don't much care," said Alice.

"Then it doesn't matter which way you go,"

said the Cat.

If we don't much care where we want to end up, it

doesn't much matter which way we go; but, like

Alice, we might end up having tea with the Mad

Hatter. Our sense of purpose is set by where we

are coming from and where we intend to go.

—Fay Angus
*Running Around
in Spiritual Circles*

You can live without someone,
if you have something to live for.

We are free up to the point of choice;
then the choice controls the chooser.

—Mary C. Crowley

*R*EACH OUT

When your own heart's been broken, it will be time for you to think of talking.

—C. S. Lewis

There are others all around you who are lonely, too. Reach out to them, because together neither of you will be lonely anymore.

Love consists in this: that two solitudes protect and touch and greet each other.

—Rainer Maria Rilke

Loneliness does not come from having no people about one, but from being unable to communicate the things that seem important to oneself.

—C. G. Jung

And he who has dwelt

with his heart alone

hears all the music

in friendship's tone.

COMING BACK

People leave. They go away for many reasons. And
we are left behind. A husband dies, and the
weeping wife is left behind to cope with aging
years alone. A mother dies, and the baby girl
whose birth brought her death is left behind
in a lonely world to struggle into adulthood.
Divorce forces one mate to leave and the other
to be left behind with feelings of rejection and
frustration. A dear friend moves away, and the
companion is left behind with hours of silence
and detachment. Even the Lord went away and
left his disciples behind staring after him into
the lonely sky.

But he is coming back! He is coming back to welcome
the widow, the orphan, the divorcee, the friend
and all his disciples into the mansions and
celebrations of heaven itself. Yes, he is coming
back! And you will never be left behind and
alone again.

When *we must be parted by death*
or distance, remember me with smiles
and laughter, for that's how I'll be
remembering you. If you can only
remember me with tears, then don't
remember me at all, for I would not
cause you sorrow. Not now.
No, not ever.

ALL HEART

But as often happens, just as a man
who has had trouble with a poor
physician fears to entrust himself even
to a good one, so it is with my heart's health.
—Adapted from Augustine

A heart that has dwelt in another's soul
does not return unchanged.

God will mend a broken heart
if we give him all the pieces.
—Unknown

Sorrow stretches out
places in the heart.
—Unknown

*O*BTOBBALARITY

*L*ife is delicious! It's got the obtobbalarity. My mom
used to say something that tasted really good
was larapin'. And I believe life is larapin' too.
In fact, it's a little bit like eating ice cream. If you
leave it in the freezer, it stays hard—too hard to
eat. You have to take it out, let it thaw out a bit,
soften it up. Then it's delightfully smooth, cool
and creamy. You can lick it off a cone a little at a
time, or you can just go after it with a big spoon
right out of the bucket. Personally, I like life
on a cone…a double dip, if you please…
so I can just eat the whole thing. It's got the
obtobbalarity, and it's larapin' good to the
last lick!

We act as though comfort and luxury

were the chief requirements of life,

when all that we need to make us really happy

is something to be enthusiastic about.

---Charles Kingsley

*W*ONDERS WITHIN

"*I* saw him (God). I did so,"
   said the child.

"We will go and look all about,"
   I comforted, "for that is good to do.
   But mostly we will look inside,
   for that is where we ache and
   where we laugh and where at last
   we die. I think it is most there
   that he is very close."

   —Loren Eiseley

We carry within us the
wonders we seek without us.

   —Sir Thomas Browne

$\mathcal{C}$ONTINUE TO CLIMB

$\mathcal{G}$oing up a mountain path one day, I met a
mountaineer with an ax in his hand. I walked
with him and asked him what he was going to
cut. "I need a piece of timber to fix my wagon,"
he said. "I need the toughest kind of wood I can
get. That kind always grows on top of the
mountain, where all the storms hit the hardest."
Storms rend and mar; but they strengthen, they
build, and they may bring forth serene and
changeless beauty. The beauty born of storms
has a nobility about it. We are prone to lament
that the world is not better. Yet, the fact that it
is full of trouble affords us our only chance to
spend our hearts. Times of storm and peril are
the ones that show what we are made of. A
storm is always a challenge; there seems to be
something in the heart that rises up to meet it.
—Unknown

Whatever the struggle,
continue the climb;
it may be only one step
to the summit.
—Diane Westlake

The world is not interested in the
storms you encountered, but
whether you brought in the ship.
—*Journal of True Education*

I'm sorry I can't heal your pain. I don't have the midas
touch to make life golden and happy ever after.
I can't make roses bloom from your despair or
rainbows appear in the dark clouds. But I can
be there when you need someone to listen.
And I'll understand, because I've been through
the same storm...and survived. You will, too.

BE YOURSELF

But at this moment I came upon myself.
Previously I had existed, too, but
everything had merely happened
to me. Now I happened to myself.
Now I knew: I am myself now;
now I exist. Previously I had
been willed to do this and that;
now I willed.
—C. G. Jung

The gospel of autonomy is that
no matter what else happens
in your life, you must be able
to live with yourself.
—Alice Slaiken Lawhead

We must be our own
before we can be another's.
—Emerson

*L*et each person therefore have confidence in the
individual nature which God had given him,
let him find there the basis for his life and
the path which is revealed to him leading
him to God; let him not suffer any image to
be imposed by somebody else or receive
any measure from outside.

—Romano Guardini

to be nobody but yourself—
in a world which is doing it best
night and day
to make you everybody else—
means to fight the hardest battle
which any human being can fight,
and never stop fighting.

—e e cummings, letter 1935

*T*HE ARTIST

*T*he great artist meticulously mixes colors to obtain
the perfect hues and tones. Then he gently
sweeps his brush here and dabs it there on
the canvas, always with the final masterpiece
in his mind's eye. He knows that great art is
composed of cheerful yellows, passionate reds
and peaceful blues and greens. But he also
recognizes that it is the more subtle purples,
greys and blacks that add depth and reality
to the picture. And so it is with the art of
your life. Happiness becomes real against
a backdrop of struggles and trials.
And the great artist sweeps and dabs his
gentle brush against the canvas of your life,
always with the final masterpiece
in mind.

Artistic paternity
is as wholesome
as physical paternity.
—G. K. Chesterton

*I*t is not my business
to think about myself.
My business is to
think about God.
It is for God to
think about me.
—Simone Weil

KEEP WALKING

Loneliness is like walking through a rain forest It's a quiet feeling. It's dark and cold, and you're alone. The underbrush is thick, and the giant trees cast eerie shadows across your path. Spider webs brush against your face. And everywhere around you…everywhere…the raindrops fall. They drip into your hair and onto your cheeks. They trickle down your arms and soak through your shoes.

But you keep on walking.

Then, from time to time, the sunshine breaks through and streams down through the darkness in brilliant rays. At first, you squint and cover your eyes. But you keep on walking. As you come closer to the edge of the forest where the trees are farther apart, the sun shines through more often, and it lifts your spirits.

Finally, you emerge into a field of sunshine and daisies. You've walked through the forest and come out into the delight of a clear day ahead. Yes, loneliness will go away, but you must keep walking toward the sunshine so that you don't become lost in the rain forest.

Some comedy
is only tragedy
plus time.
—Carol Burnett

*C*ALL ME

When you are tempted to be low and
     despondent, if such feelings ever
     come on you, as if you were lonely
     and desolate, do recollect that
     there is one at a distance who is
     thinking of you and praying for
     you; and into whose eyes tears
     start at the thought of your
     having any sorrow or perplexity.

—John Henry Newman

If you're too proud
(or too afraid)
to admit you are
hurting, don't be
surprised if nobody
seems to care.

—Robert Schuller

ALONE WITH GOD

I enter into the presence
of God with all my load of
misery and troubles. And
he takes me just as I am
and makes me to be alone
with him.

—Raissa Maritain

That perfect silence is where the
lips and heart are still, and we
no longer entertain our own
imperfect thoughts and vain
opinions…But God alone
speaks in us, and we wait
in singleness of heart.

—Henry Wadsworth Longfellow

𝒯EDDY BEAR

. . . .

I remember when I was brand new and came here to
live. My make believe fur was soft and fluffy; my
nose was shiny and black; and my plastic button
eyes gleamed when the light hit them. I had on
a big red bow, and when you pulled the string at
the back of my neck, I said, "I love you." I had a
nice smile that made everyone want to pick me
up and hug me tight. And I was the center of
attention in my spot on the bed leaning against
the pillows.

As time went by, though, my newness wore off.
Sometimes I was left lying in the cold corner.
My ribbon faded from the sunlight, and the dog
chewed up one of my ears.

My nose came loose, and the baby pulled off one of
my eyes. My smile was a little crooked, and my
fur got dirty. Nobody paid much attention to me
then, and I rarely ever got a hug anymore.
Worst of all, something went wrong inside of

me, and when they pulled my string I couldn't say, "I love you" anymore.

Then one day some kind, gentle hands picked me up out of the corner. They brushed my fur until it was soft and fluffy again. They sewed my nose back on and stitched up my tattered ear. They glued on a new eye and straightened out my smile. Then they tied a bright, new yellow ribbon around my neck. But, best of all, they gently replaced my batteries, tugged on the new string they had sewn at the back of my neck, and I heard my little voice crackle, "I love you."

Then, the most wonderful thing happened. Those gentle hands picked me up and handed me to a child with a big smile and outstretched arms. And it was love at first sight. Little hands stroked my fur, squeezed me and hugged me tight.

Thank you, Lord, for picking me up, putting me back together and loving me just as if I am brand new.

*P*EACE

. . . .

I saw him again today, Lord,

Just a glimpse,

in a crowded street,

But it was enough…

Enough to open the wounds again

To allow the bitter memories

of those hard words,

broken promises and the mistakes I made,

to come flooding back.

I almost got caught, Lord.

Caught in a wave of self pity,

self recrimination and guilt.

And then I remembered…

Remembered that failure

brought to you and confessed,

Is failure forgiven,

forgotten, dealt with.

So now I can look back

to that experience—

thankful for lessons learned.

I can look up to you—confident

that you can create beauty

out of the ashes of my mistakes.

I can look forward

to the future—at peace.

—Marion Stroud
Celebrate Friendship

True peace doesn't come from

the absence of trouble. It comes

from the presence of God.

—Unknown

LOVE YOURSELF

Love yourself last. Look around and see what
your duty is to those who walk beside
you down life's road. Make their days
happy with little acts of beauty. And help
them carry their heavy loads.

Love yourself last. Look for the stranger who
staggers under his despair and
loneliness. Go, lend him a hand. Help
him to a higher place in life where he
may be able to see a fairer world.

Love yourself last. And you will grow in spirit.
You will see new things. You will hear
new songs. You will know things you
never imagined. And you will understand
the deeper meanings of life. You will
hear the messages of the stars. And all
God's joys will be at your very command.

Love yourself last. And, oh, what joy will thrill

you! It is a thrill that selfish souls will

never know. Peace will fill your heart,

and earth will seem like just an ante-

chamber to heaven.

Love yourself last. Then, you will truly

love yourself best.

—Unknown

*B*EING THERE

Sometimes I pray to you, Lord, but it seems my
   prayer just bounces off the ceiling in my room
   and doesn't rise to your hearing. I read your
   precious word and, yet, my mind's in another
   world, and the words just stick to the page.
   I long to be with you, talk to you, listen to you,
   but all I feel is alone.
Other times, when I least expect it, a friend gives me
   a warm hug, and I feel your arms around me.
   I hear you whisper, "I love you, my child" in the
   wind. Or a butterfly lightly lands on a nearby
   flower and lets me know that you're there with
   me all the time. The ocean laps gently against
   the sand and washes away the footprints of
   trouble and despair. And your wildflowers
   proclaim happiness in a rainbow of brilliant
   blooms that lighten my heart and fill my soul
   with hope and trust. Thanks for being there,
   Lord.

Friendship does not

commit the supreme treason:

failure to be there

when you're needed.

You

You cannot be given a life
by someone else. Of all the
people you will know in your
lifetime, you are the only one
you will never leave nor lose.
To the questions of your life,
you are the only answer.
To the problems of your life,
you are the only solution.

—Unknown

*C*OME TO PASS

"*I*t has come to pass." God's word says it so often. Perhaps, it's because the Lord knew that if trouble came to stay we could not survive. And there are times when you may feel the excruciating pain will never pass. But it does. Life goes on…and so must we. So, when the pain seems endless, unbearable and there seems to be no light at the end of the tunnel, remember that God himself has promised that "it has come to pass."

We are not primarily put
on this earth to see
through one another, but
to see one another through.

—Peter De Vries

*T*AKE THE RISK

*T*o love at all is to be vulnerable. Love anything, and your heart will certainly be wrung and possibly be broken. If you want to make sure of keeping it intact, you must give your heart to no one, not even to an animal. Wrap it carefully round with hobbies and little luxuries; avoid all entanglements; lock it up safe in the casket or coffin of your selfishness. But in that casket—safe, dark, motionless, airless—it will change. It will not be broken; it will become unbreakable, impenetrable, irredeemable. The alternative to tragedy, or at least to the risk of tragedy, is damnation. The only place outside Heaven where you can be perfectly safe from all the dangers and perturbations of love is Hell.

—C. S. Lewis

Love is risky business—
you risk your heart,
your love, your pride,
your time and hope
and dreams to the
imperfection of
someone else.
—Unknown

Love is always willing
to give and take risks.
It's like Johnson grass!
It's robust,
it has guts,
it's tenacious.
—Unknown

*P*RAY

*T*he life of prayer is perhaps the most mysterious of
all human experience. We come to be at home
with a God we cannot see. We discover that it is
only by giving ourselves away totally that we
truly come to possess ourselves, that we are
most free when most surrendered. We begin to
realize that light is darkness and darkness light.
We become lost in a trackless desert—and then,
if we persevere despite our disorientation, we
begin to realize that it is only in being lost, in
losing ourselves, that we are found. The whole
of our life, and not just our prayer life, becomes
a paradox, an apparent contradiction concealing
and revealing a deeper truth, because we begin
to realize that we must live as we pray.

—Thomas Green

*B*ELIEVE

These, then, are my
last words to you:
Be not afraid of life.
Believe that life is
worth living,
and your belief will
help create the fact.

—William James
"The Will to Believe"